21

First Facts™

Community Helpers at Work

A Day in the Life of a
Construction Worker

by Heather Adamson

Consultant:
Ronald J. Ramos
Executive Vice President
ConstructionJobs.com
Encinitas, California

Capstone
press

Mankato, Minnesota

First Facts is published by Capstone Press
151 Good Counsel Drive, P.O. Box 669, Mankato, Minnesota 56002
http://www.capstonepress.com

Library of Congress Cataloging-in-Publication Data
Adamson, Heather, 1974–
    A day in the life of a construction worker/by Heather Adamson.
       p. cm.—(First facts. Community helpers at work)
    Includes bibliographical references and index.
    Contents: When do construction workers start their days?—What do construction
workers do?—Do construction workers work alone?—How do construction workers stay
safe?—Where do construction workers eat lunch?—Who helps construction workers?—
How do construction workers know what to build?—What happens at the end of a
construction worker's day?—Amazing but true!
    ISBN 0-7368-2505-3 (hardcover)
    1. Building—Juvenile literature. [1. Construction workers. 2. Building. 3. Occupations.]
I. Title. II. Series.
TH149.A337 2003
690'.023—dc21   2003011453

Editorial Credits
Jennifer Bergstrom, series designer; Enoch Peterson, book designer; Gary Sundermeyer,
    photographer; Eric Kudalis, product planning editor

Photo Credits
Capstone Press/Gary Sundermeyer, cover, 1, 5, 7, 8–9, 10, 12–13, 14, 15, 16–17, 19, 20–21
Corbis/Royalty Free, 6
Corel, 20 (inset)

Artistic Effects
Comstock, EyeWire/Photodisc, Stockbyte

Capstone Press thanks Brad Bohlen for his help in photographing this book.

1 2 3 4 5 6 09 08 07 06 05 04

Table of Contents

When do construction workers start their days?

Most construction workers start their days early in the morning. They like to work outside while it is cool and light. Brad is in charge of many workers and projects. He goes to his office before heading to the job sites.

Fun Fact:

In 2002, more than 6.5 million people worked construction jobs in the United States.

5:30 in the
morning

5

What do construction workers do?

Construction workers do different tasks. Some build roads. Other workers build homes or offices. Construction workers dig, pound, cut, and measure.

Do construction workers work alone?

Construction workers work together in **crews**. Brad checks to make sure this **foundation** crew has enough people for the job. A driver backs up the concrete truck. Another worker moves the **chute**. The rest of the crew spreads the concrete with shovels and **trowels**.

Fun Fact:
Concrete is the most-used construction material in the world. More concrete is used than all other building materials combined.

9:30 in the morning

9

How do construction workers stay safe?

Construction workers use clothing and equipment to stay safe. Brad wears strong boots to protect his feet. He wears a hard hat while he checks supplies at the job site. The **framing crew** uses safety glasses when they cut boards. They use ear plugs to soften the noise from saws and hammers.

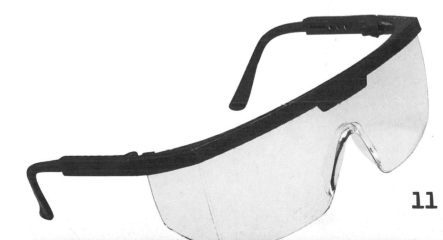

12:30 in the afternoon

Fun Fact:

One portable toilet can accommodate 10 construction workers for a week before it needs to be emptied.

Where do construction workers eat lunch?

Most construction workers eat lunch at the job site. Some bring packed lunches. Others buy their meals from a lunch truck. Brad gives cold water to everyone. Without enough water, workers could get **heatstroke**.

13

Who helps construction workers?

Many people help construction workers. **Architects** and designers help by drawing plans. Contractors run construction projects.

Inspectors also help construction
workers. They check the work to make
sure it meets city building codes. An
inspector helps Brad check that the roof
is safe and waterproof.

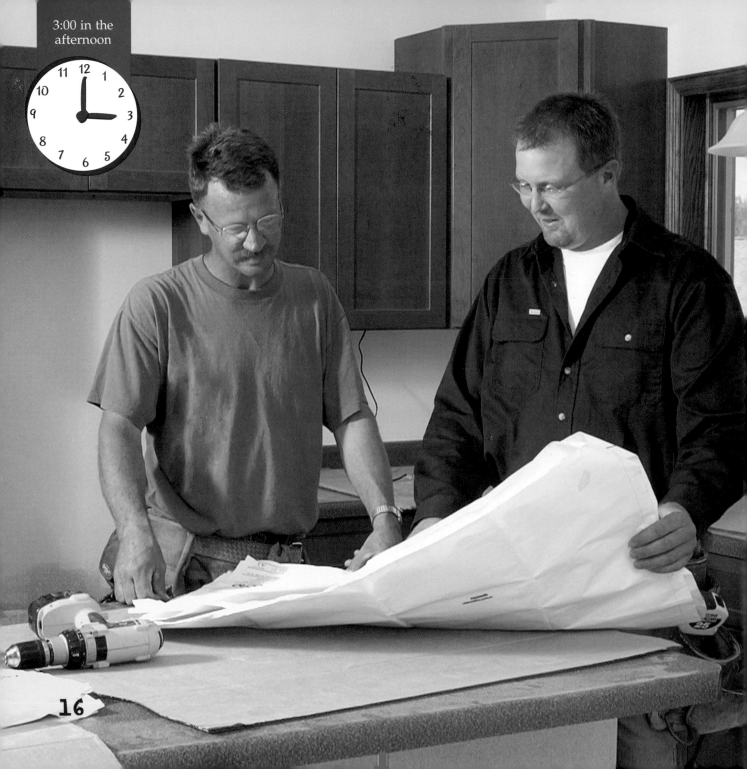

3:00 in the afternoon

16

How do construction workers know what to build?

Construction workers follow plans. The plans tell workers how to build things. Brad reads the plans for this kitchen. He makes sure the crew follows the plans exactly. He checks if there is enough space for the sink.

What happens at the end of a construction worker's day?

Before construction workers leave, they make sure the job site is clean and safe. The crew loads garbage into a bin. They sweep up any nails left on the road and sidewalk. Brad piles siding neatly. He checks tomorrow's schedule before heading home.

19

The Great Wall of China is one of the world's longest construction projects. It is about 4,000 miles (6,400 kilometers) long. Work began on the Great Wall about 2,500 years ago.

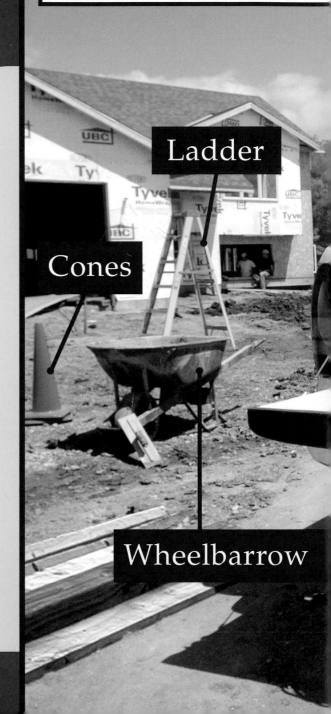

Ladder

Cones

Wheelbarrow

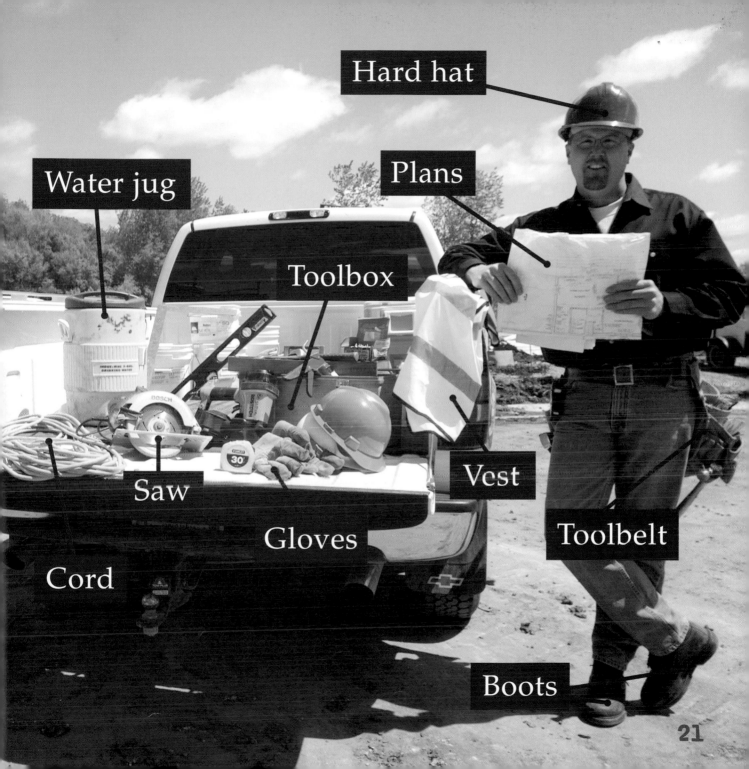

Hard hat

Water jug

Plans

Toolbox

Saw

Vest

Gloves

Cord

Toolbelt

Boots

Glossary

architect (AR-ki-tekt)—a person who draws plans that show how buildings should be built

chute (SHOOT)—a narrow, tilted passage through which objects may pass

crew (KROO)—a team of people who work together

foundation (foun-DAY-shuhn)—a solid base on which a structure is built

framing crew (FRAYM-ing KROO)—a team of people who put together the basic structure of a building

heatstroke (HEET STROHK)—a serious illness caused by working in the heat too long

trowel (TROU-uhl)—a hand tool with a flat blade; trowels are used for laying concrete and plastering walls.

Read More

Hayward, Linda. *A Day in the Life of a Builder.* Dorling Kindersley Readers. New York: Dorling Kindersley, 2001.

Schaefer, Lola M. *Construction Site.* Who Works Here? Chicago: Heinemann, 2000.

Internet Sites

FactHound offers a safe, fun way to find Internet sites related to this book. All of the sites on FactHound have been researched by our staff.

Here's how:
1. Visit *www.facthound.com*
2. Type in this special code **0736825053** for age-appropriate sites. Or enter a search word related to this book for a more general search.
3. Click on the Fetch It button.

FactHound will fetch the best sites for you!

Index